ARCHES TO ZIGZAGS

An Architecture ABC

Verse by Michael J. Crosbie

Photography by Steve and Kit Rosenthal

Harry N. Abrams, Inc., Publishers

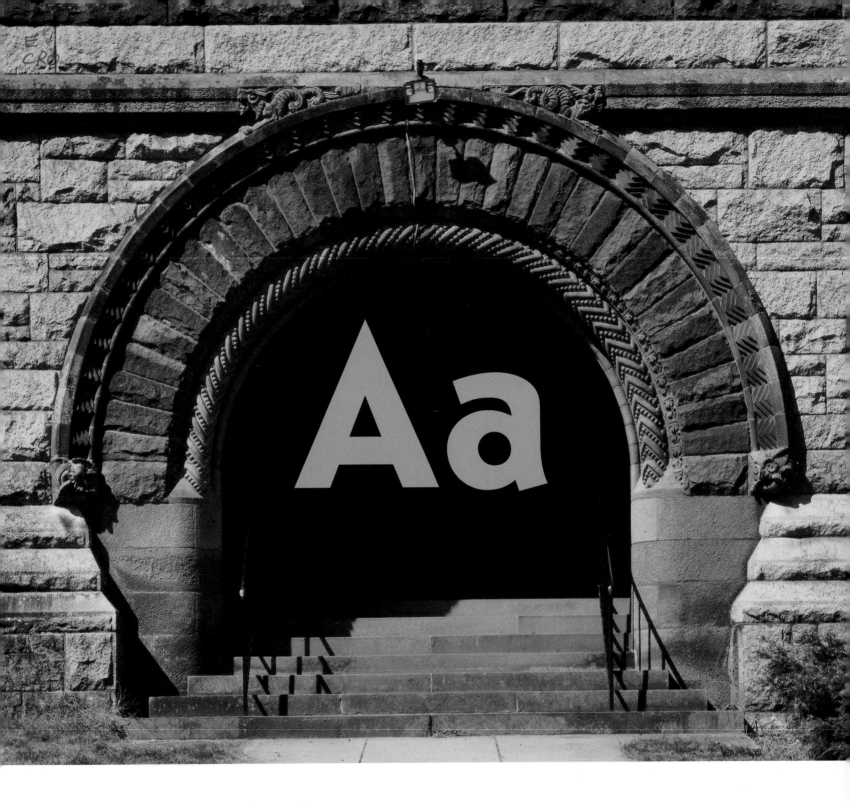

A is for Arch

A big, yawning mouth
Welcomes people inside.
Do you know a building
That opens so wide?

Bb

B is for Balcony

A perch way up high
To spy far and near.
When you look from a balcony
What sights will appear?

Cc

C is for Capital

Crowning a column
With corn, leaves, and wheat.
Does this fancy capital
Look good enough to eat?

Dd

D is for Double Door

Two doors make a double
In blues dark and pale.
Which one has a knob?
Which one is for mail?

Ee

E is for Eave

Look under a roof
For eaves broad and plain.
Can eaves give you shelter
From the sun and the rain?

Ff

F is for Finial

Fancy carved ornaments
Where pointy roofs stop.
How many do you see
At this house's tip-top?

G is for Gargoyle

Goblins on buildings
Who perch way up high.
Do these ugly critters
Look ready to fly?

Hh

H is for Hinge

These metal parts help
To swing doors or a gate.
Can you find four hinges
Curled up like a snake?

I is for I-beam

It's steel and it's heavy
To make a strong frame.
Can you guess how the I-beam
Got its capital name?

J is for Joist

They hold up your house
Inside ceilings and floors.
Are joists a lot like
That skeleton of yours?

Kk

K is for Keystone

The stone in the middle
Holds this arch in place.
Does it look a bit
Like a tooth in your face?

Ll

L is for Log Cabin

Logs stacked for walls
Make a cabin of trees.
How many do you think
To build one of these?

Mm

M is for Mantel

Carved wood surrounds
This fireplace pretty.
What would you put there
Besides a glass kitty?

Nn

N is for Neon

Bright light that glows
From gas in glass pipes.
What colors would you add
To these juicy stripes?

O is for Obelisk

A towering needle
Made of stone by the ton.
Do you know what obelisk
Is named "Washington"?

P p

P is for Porch

Places to sit
With friends by the pack.
Is a porch on your house
In the front or the back?

Q is for Quoin

Placed at the corner
For strength like a rock.
Could you climb this ladder
Of block upon block?

Rr

R is for Ruin

A building worn down
By wind, rain, and time.
Can you picture this ruin
Before its decline?

Ss

S is for Silo

A proud tower stands
On a farm on the plain.
What would you store here?
Corn, wheat, oats, or grain?

Tt

T is for Turret

A curved, painted spire
With rooms in the round.
If you look for a corner
Could it ever be found?

U is for Urn

A jar with a lid
Atop a fine base.
Where do you spy urns
At this elegant place?

V is for Vent

A hole in the wall
To bring fresh air through.
Could this vent be home
To a small bird or two?

W w

W is for Widow's Walk

Between two brick chimneys
With railings of white.
What might you see
From this roof top site?

X is for X-bracing

X marks the spot
On a skyscraper tall.
Without this strong bracing
Do you think it might fall?

Y is for Yard

Some houses have yards
In the back, front, or side.
If this were your yard
Just where would you hide?

Z is for Zigzag

Up, down, and up
Zigs a zag of pastel.
Goes right or goes left?
Which way? Can you tell?

What is Architecture?

If you look in a dictionary for the word "architecture," you'll find that it means "the art and science of erecting buildings." But like a dictionary itself, architecture covers lots of things, from A to Z.

Architecture is all around us. You can find architecture nearly everywhere you look—in houses and hotels, schools and stores, temples and towers, nurseries and neighborhoods. An element of architecture can be really big (like a supertall obelisk) or really small (like a single door hinge). In this book you'll find architecture in cities and way out in the country, in places old and new, and in all shapes and sizes, colors and textures.

Because you spend so much time in it, around it, and next to it, you might want to know some of the things that architecture is made of—like arches and capitals, gargoyles and quoins, turrets and zigzags. You can probably find many of these architectural elements wherever you go—the buildings you visit, even in your own house or school. Look around right this minute—what parts of architecture can you find?

A is for Arch
An arch is a rounded or curved opening in a wall or between columns. It can be made of any material, but is usually of stone or brick. This arch is on the Ames Free Library in North Easton, Massachusetts, designed by Henry Hobson Richardson, and built in 1877.

B is for Balcony
A balcony is a platform, accessible from a door or window, that projects from the face of a building. It is usually on the second floor or above and is enclosed with a railing. This balcony is on the Santa Barbara County Courthouse in Santa Barbara, California, designed by William Mooser III, and built in 1929.

C is for Capital
A capital is found at the top of a column in classical architecture and is often decorated with elaborate ornament. This corncob capital is on Alumni Hall, University of North Carolina, Chapel Hill, North Carolina, designed by A. J. Davis around 1850.

D is for Double Door
A double door is made up of two separate swinging doors (also known as leafs) that are hung in a single door frame. A double door is usually the main entrance to a building, such as this one, which is on a house in San Francisco, California, built in 1895 by Matthew Kavanaugh.

E is for Eave
An eave is the underside of a roof, either sloped or flat, that extends beyond the outside wall of a building. These gigantic eaves are on the Frederick C. Robie house in Chicago, Illinois, designed by Frank Lloyd Wright, and built in 1909.

F is for Finial

A finial is an ornamental object, usually made of wood or stone, that terminates the peak of a sloped roof or a spire. These finials are on the Fernald House in Santa Barbara, California, designed by Thomas Nixon and built in 1862. The finials were added when the house was remodeled in 1880, the design of which is attributed to Roswell Forbush.

G is for Gargoyle

A gargoyle is a grotesque creature, usually carved in stone, that decorates the exterior of a building, most often located near the roof eave. The oldest gargoyles are found on Gothic churches built 700 or 800 years ago and serve as waterspouts for the building's gutter system. These gargoyles are on the Hull Biological Labs building at the University of Chicago, designed by Henry Ives Cobb in 1897.

H is for Hinge

A hinge is a device, usually of metal, that connects a door to a door frame. Hinge plates, which are fastened to the door and the frame, are joined with a pin, which allows the door to swing. Hinges can be simple or ornamental, as they are on the Trinity Episcopal Church in York Harbor, Maine, designed by J. H. Hardenburgh, and constructed in 1908.

I is for I-beam

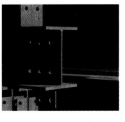

An I-beam is a structural part of a building, made of steel. It connects to other I-beams and pieces of steel (usually with bolts) to create a framework, which is then covered with floors and walls. This I-beam was photographed at the Novel Iron Works in Greenland, New Hampshire.

J is for Joist

A joist, like an I-beam, is part of a building's structure. Joists are usually made of wood or light steel and are used to support floors and ceilings. They are often covered with materials and hidden from view. These joists are in a house under construction in Newton, Massachusetts.

K is for Keystone

The keystone is one of the most important parts of an arch. It is always found at the very top and is usually shaped like a wedge. It is the last piece placed when building an arch and holds all of the other bricks or stones in place. This keystone is on the Rotunda Library at the University of Virginia in Charlottesville, Virginia, designed by Thomas Jefferson, and built in 1826.

L is for Log Cabin

A log cabin is made of tree trunks stacked on top of each other. The corners are notched so that the logs overlap. This one is found at the Lincoln Log Cabin State Historic Site in Charleston, Illinois, and is a replica of the home of Abraham Lincoln's father, Thomas, occupied between 1840 and 1851.

M is for Mantel

A mantel is the decorative woodwork or stonework that frames the opening of a fireplace—especially the shelf over the opening. This mantel is in a house built in 1892 in Newton Centre, Massachusetts.

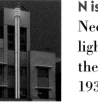

N is for Neon

Neon is a gas used in glass tubes that glows when electricity runs through it. Neon lights, which can be made in any color, are often used to light up a building because the tubes can be bent to trace its outlines. This neon is on a building built in the 1930s in the Art Deco district in South Beach, Miami Beach, Florida.

O is for Obelisk

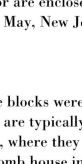

An obelisk is a tall shaft of stone usually with four sides that becomes narrower as it goes up. The top is pointed like a needle. This obelisk is the Washington Monument in Washington, D.C., designed in 1836 by Robert Mills.

P is for Porch

A porch is attached to the outside of a building and usually surrounds an entrance. Porches sometimes have roofs and railings or are enclosed with metal screens or glass. This porch is on the John Wesley Inn, Cape May, New Jersey, built in 1872 by Stephen Button.

Q is for Quoin

Quoins are found at the corners of buildings. These large blocks were originally placed to strengthen a building's corners, but today they are typically more ornamental than structural, such as in wooden buildings, where they are purely decoration. These wooden quoins are on the Joseph Titcomb house in Kennebunk, Maine, designed by Gridley James Fox Bryant, and built in 1855.

R is for Ruin

A ruin is a building, usually an old one, that has fallen apart. Some ruins are the result of fires, floods, or earthquakes. But a ruin can be simply a building that has been abandoned, with no one to care for it. This ruin is at the Wupatki National Monument in Arizona, which was occupied by Native Americans, circa 1120–1210.

S is for Silo

A silo is a storage building on a farm, usually made of concrete blocks, wood, or metal. Grain is poured through a door at the top and removed through a door at the bottom. This silo is on a farm in Arthur, Illinois.

T is for Turret

A turret is a "minitower," usually round and located at the corner of a building. It often has a single, circular room on each floor. This turret is on the Milton Carson house in Eureka, California, built in 1889.

U is for Urn

An urn is used to decorate the outside or inside of a building. Old buildings have urns made of wood or stone, but today urns can be made of plastic and look just like the old ones. These old urns are on the McLellan House at the Portland Museum of Art in Portland, Maine, designed by John Kimball, Sr., and built in 1801.

V is for Vent

A vent is an opening in a building wall, usually up near the top of the roof, that allows fresh air to circulate into an attic. This vent is on the Four Seasons Biltmore Hotel in Montecito, California, designed by Reginald Johnson, and built in 1927.

W is for Widow's Walk

A widow's walk is a platform surrounded by railings at the top of a house. It is so named because it was used by the wife of a sea captain to watch for the return of her husband's ship. Sometimes the captain never came back. This widow's walk is on the Andrew-Safford house at the Peabody Essex Museum in Salem, Massachusetts, built in 1819.

X is for X-bracing

X-bracing is used to strengthen the frame of tall buildings, extending from corner to corner. This bracing is on the John Hancock Center in Chicago, Illinois, designed by Skidmore, Owings & Merrill and constructed in 1969.

Y is for Yard

A yard is an open space, usually bounded by landscaping, fences, or the exterior walls of a building. This yard is at the Mary and Edward Allen house in Natick, Massachusetts, and was designed by Thomas Wirth in 1989.

Z is for Zigzag

A zigzag is an ornament usually found at the top of buildings. Zigzags were very popular during the Art Deco period. This zigzag is on a building from the Art Deco district in South Beach, Miami Beach, Florida, which was built in the 1930s.

Acknowledgments

The authors are grateful to a number of people who helped to make this book possible:
Edward Allen, George Campbell, Jane Cohn, Brigit Rose Crosbie, Claire Gallagher,
Michael Lapides, Susan Maguire, Edward Miller, Howard Reeves and Lia Ronnen at
Harry N. Abrams, Inc., Liza Rosenthal, and Stephanie Spinner.

Designer: Ed Miller

Library of Congress Cataloging-in-Publication Data

Crosbie, Michael J.
    Arches to zigzags : an architecture abc / Michael J. Crosbie, Steve and Kit Rosenthal.
      p. cm.
    Summary: A rhyming alphabet of architectural elements, from arches and doors to I-beams, mantels, and urns.
    ISBN 0-8109-4218-6 (hc)
      1. Architecture—Details—Juvenile literature. 2. Alphabet rhymes.
[1. Architecture. 2. Alphabet.] I. Rosenthal, Steve, 1940– II. Rosenthal, Kit. III. Title.

    NA2840 .C74 2000
    721—dc21   99-89643

Printed and bound in Hong Kong

Harry N. Abrams, Inc.
100 Fifth Avenue
New York, N.Y. 10011
www.abramsbooks.com